CHRISTMAS PROGRAM BUILDER

No. 35

Plays—Pantomimes—Songs
Recitations—Exercises

Compiled by Paul M. Miller

For the most practical use of this material, it is suggested the group using the booklet obtain at least three copies: one to be used by the director, and the others to be clipped for those participat-in the program.

Litho in U.S.A.

Lillenas Publishing Co.
KANSAS CITY, MO. 64141

GRADED PROGRAM MATERIAL

Ages 3-5

I'm Little Now

I'm little now,
But I can bow, *(bows)*
And I can say,
"God bless your way!"
(bows again)

—Dorothy Conant Stroud

Christmas Farewell

Thank you for coming
To our program today.
Now please listen closely,
And hear what we say . . .
(*Whole group shouts:*
"Merry Christmas!")

—P. M. Miller

You're Welcome

I can't say a big piece—
I'm little, you see;
I'll just say you're welcome
As welcome can be!

—Dorothy Conant Stroud

Jesus' Happy Birthday

(To be recited by one member of the kindergarten class before the whole group plays their rhythm band instruments.)

This is Jesus' happy birthday,
And it's a very special time.
Now our children's band says,
"Welcome!"
With rhythm sticks and bells that
chime.

—Anna Marie Dahlquist

Door to Our Hearts

Dear Jesus, we thank Thee for coming
To earth to save us from sin;
We open the doors of our hearts today,
And gladly welcome Thee in!

—Rega Kramer McCarty

For Everyone

Christmas is for everyone,
As God meant it to be.
Jesus is for everyone,
And that means you and me!

—Cora M. Owen

Living Christmas

Living and giving
Is Christmas living.

Showing and telling—
That's Christmas dwelling.

Shining and glowing—
That's Christmas showing.

—Cora M. Owen

At Christmastime

(To be recited by a small child, held by a father who has an open Bible.)

At Christmastime
I love to climb
Upon my daddy's knee;
And hear again
Of Bethlehem,
While Daddy reads to me.

—Anna Marie Dahlquist

Please Join Us

I wish a wish this Christmas,
That all of you out there,
Join us in our worship,
In thought and song and prayer.

—Rega Kramer McCarty

You Can, Too!

I'm so very glad I came!
Aren't you?
I can praise our Savior's name—
You can, too!

—Dorothy Conant Stroud

Blessed Story

The bells ring out so loud and clear,
They tell us Christmas brings good cheer.
The story of a Child so dear
Is heard again both far and near.

—Gladys M. Seiders

The Belles of Christmas

(An exercise for four girls. Each carries a bell, which she rings before speaking.)

1st Girl—
Ring a bell on Christmas morn,
To tell the news that Christ is born.

2nd Girl—
My ringing bell tells the world,
Jesus came for each boy and girl.

3rd Girl—
Angels had no bell to ring,
So their message did they sing.

4th Girl—
Bells and songs are for this day;
Around the manger let us pray.

All Girls—
We ring our bells, and say with joy,
On Christmas Day God sent His Boy.

—Paula Medford

A Song for Christmas

Of all the times, in all the year,
It's Christmastime we hold most dear.

Of all the days, the whole year long,
It's Christmas Day that gives our song.

(Children's group sings.)

—P. M. Miller

A Boy's Gift

(Boy enters, dressed as a shepherd. He carries a toy lamb.)

If I were a shepherd,
I know what I'd do;
I'd give Jesus my lamb.
And be His friend too.

(Modern boy enters. He carries a wrapped gift.)

Since I'm not a shepherd,
Or a wise man, or king;
I'll give Him myself,
My life I will bring.

—Timothy Miller

Christmas Love

1st Child—
Boys and girls love gifts and toys,

2nd Child—
And all the other Christmas joys.

3rd Child—
But most of all, we love the child,

4th Child—
Who came to earth all meek and mild.

5th Child—
Jesus was that baby Boy,

6th Child—
The Son of God, who brings us joy.

—Naomi E. Allen

GRADED PROGRAM MATERIAL | **Ages 6-8**

The Best Gift

1st Child—

I got a doll named Tessie—
I want you all to see! *(hold high)*
I show my love for Tessie *(hugs)*
As Mother's love for me!

2nd Child—

I got a ball for bouncing! *(bounces it)*
I really think it's neat!
But I must be so careful
And keep it off the street!

3rd Child—

I got a horn for blowing,
And it has quite a beep! *(blows it)*
But I must never blow it
When baby is asleep!

4th Child—

I got a game for playing *(shows game)*.
It's one that's quite well known.
But now I'd like to share it.
It isn't fun alone!

Unison—

Be thankful for the gifts you get;
Tho' some are large and some are small.
When God gave us His only Son,
He was the greatest gift of all!

—E. L. Russell

Jesus Came to Earth

(An exercise for four primary children. Optional pantomimes can make it the entire departmental presentation.)

(Pantomine the manger scene.)

1st Child—

Jesus came to earth one day,
Came to take my sins away.
He was born in manger bed,
Even as the Bible said.

2nd Child—*(Angels enter and go to the manger.)*

Angels from the realms on high
Showed their glory in the sky.
They proclaimed the news to earth;
Announced the news of Jesus' birth.

3rd Child—*(Shepherds join angels.)*

Shepherds saw the heavenly sight,
Heard the gladsome news that night.
Left their flocks and came to see—
Knelt and worshipped on their knee.

4th Child—*(As wise men enter.)*

Wise men traveled from afar,
Followed closely heavenly star.
In their hands their gifts they bring,
Give them to the newborn King.

Unison *or one child each line*—

We today should worship, too.
It's the nicest thing to do.
Of Jesus' coming we will sing—
Our talents, gifts, we'll gladly bring!

—E. L. Russell

Little Baby Jesus

Little Baby Jesus,
Child so pure and sweet.
Shepherds came to see Him,
Came the Lord to greet.

Little Baby Jesus,
He was God's own Son;
Came to be our Savior,
Precious holy One.

—Cora M. Owen

Secrets

The Christmas lights are shining
bright,
The gifts are underneath the tree;
Inside each one are secret things—
I do not know what's there for me!

But this I know, that God's best gift
Is surely NOT a secret thing!
He gave His dear Son, Jesus Christ,
To be our Savior and our King.

—Anna Marie Dahlquist

God's Christmas Gift

God's gift was not a pretty package
'Neath a tinseled Christmas tree;
But a baby, warm and loving,
Before whom wise men bowed the
knee!

—Grace Richie

That Star

(For four small children, each holding a star.)

That star
So far away and bright,

That star
Which filled the sky with light,

That star
Which acted as a guide,

That star
Led wise men to His side.

—Cora M. Owen

Hands at Christmas

(Four children surround a manger, dressed as the people they represent. As they recite, they show their hands to the audience.)

MARY—I'm Mary; my hands bring warmth and love
To the Baby that God sent from heaven above.

JOSEPH—I'm Joseph; my hands are firm and strong;
They'll build Him a cradle later on.

SHEPHERD—I'm a shepherd; my hands are weathered and
bent,
But I'll fold them to worship the Savior God sent.

WISE MAN—I'm a wise man; my hands carry gold and
perfume
To the infant Redeemer, who'll save us from
doom.

UNISON—We all use our hands to honor the King,
To show Him our love, and our offerings to bring.

—Anna Marie Dahlquist

The Message of the Bells

1st Child—
What is the message of the bells?

2nd Child—
Mine *(taps bell sharply)* says "Be Quiet!"
And all children must sit down
For our teacher deserves respect—Right?

1st Child—
What is the message of the bells?

3rd Child—
Mine were used long ago
When my great-grandparents
Traveled in a sleigh over the snow.

1st Child—
What is the message of the bells?

4th Child—
Mine tells the farmer each day
Where the cows are grazing
And if one has wandered away.

1st Child—
What is the message of the bells?

5th Child—
Mine rings loud and steady
Telling all the family
That dinner now is ready.

6th Child—
One bell we could not carry
It's up there in the steeple
(points to where church bell is located)

Unison—
It rings out the Christmas joy
For all of God's good people!

—Helen Kitchell Evans

The Animals

(As the children recite, have them place flannelgraph figures around the manger scene on a flannel board.)

A tired donkey in a barn
Saw Jesus' face at early morn.

A fleecy lamb all wet with dew
Heard angels say, "Christ's born to you!"

A camel weary from the road
Saw where our Lord made His abode.

And all became as glad as could be
For God's great gift to you and me.

—Anna Marie Dahlquist

O Holy Night

(An exercise for 10 children. Each carries a letter, spelling "O Holy Night," behind his back, holding it up as he speaks.)

O—One winter's night the shepherds came

H—Herding their sheep towards a distant flame.

O—Over a stable near Bethlehem,

L—Lending its brilliance like a gem,

Y—Yea, a great star shed its holy light;

N—No other star was quite so bright!

I—It glowed and, never seeming to dim,

G—Guided the wise men and shepherds to Him.

H—Heavenly hosts announced that morn

T—That Mary's Child, God's Son was born!

—Gladys M. Seiders

The Littlest Christmas Tree

By Jean Soule and Mildred Johnson

(Six children dressed in green, one quite small, representing Christmas trees, or holding posterboard trees of varied sizes before them.)

BIGGEST CHILD—I'm sure to be picked to trim the town hall.
The rest of you are way too small!

2ND CHILD—But I'm big enough for a schoolroom, you see.
When the children come, they'll all pick me!

3RD CHILD—Pooh! I'll be chosen to go to church—
Some of you will be left in the lurch!

4TH CHILD—I'm just the right size for a fine, rich boy;
To a wealthy girl I'll bring much joy!

5TH CHILD—I'm not the biggest, but I'm just right
For someone special on Christmas night.

SMALLEST CHILD *(tiny voice)*—But I'll be left here all alone!
I'm stunted and crooked, and undergrown!

(Two woodcutters enter, who pretend to cut down all the trees, one by one. They carry them off, leaving the littlest tree.)

SMALLEST CHILD—Oh dear! I was right! My friends were chopped down
And hauled away to the nearest town!
They'll make someone happy on Christmas Day,
With stars on their tops, and in tinsel array.
But I'm shivering here on this lonely hill.
Ah-choo! I'm afraid I'm getting a chill!

(Enter two shabbily dressed children, looking around.)

1ST CHILD—Look! Someone has cut all the trees on this lot.

2ND CHILD—But here's a tiny one, left on this spot!

1ST CHILD—It looks sad and lonesome standing here.
Let's take it home for our Christmas cheer.

2ND CHILD—We'll make some ornaments and you'll see—
We'll soon have the prettiest Christmas tree!

(Children pick up tree and carry it off together, one holding the shoulders of the little child, the other the feet.)

LITTLEST TREE *(as it's carried off)*—I may be scrawny, I may be small—
But now I'm the happiest of them all!

The Best Gift of All

By Jean Soule and Mildred Johnson

Scene—

A living room on Christmas Eve. Decorated tree with gifts.

Characters—

MOTHER (Perhaps teacher or department supervisor)
FOUR CHILDREN

1ST CHILD—I'm getting new skates, and a bicycle, too!

2ND CHILD—I'll have stacks of toys before Christmas is through!

3RD CHILD—On Christmas morning I'll have a new doll.

4TH CHILD—My gift will be the biggest of all!

1ST CHILD—How I love Christmas—It's so much fun
With dozens of presents for everyone!

(Mother enters, watches and listens a moment as children examine the gifts.)

MOTHER—I'm very concerned! I'm ashamed of you!
All of your thoughts are on gifts that are new—
Bicycles, dollies, or games and books—
I never saw such self-centered looks
As you now have on your smiling faces!
What would you do if you had to change places
With some poor child who had nothing at all?
No toys, no games, no secondhand doll?

2ND CHILD—Why, that could never happen to us!

3RD CHILD—And if it did, I'd make a fuss!

4TH CHILD *(looking ashamed)*—
Oh, Mother, you're right! How selfish we are!
We've forgotten the message of the Star! *(Points to top of tree)*

MOTHER *(smiling now)*—I'm glad that one of my children cares!
Christmas is better if someone shares.
And Someone has given of himself, you see.
That's the Christmas message for you and me.
God gave us a gift on Christmas morn—
His very own Son—this child was born
In Bethlehem, in a lowly stall.
And He is the very best gift of all.

1st Child—Should we give Him gifts?
I could find Him a train.

2nd Child—I wouldn't miss a ball or a plane.

3rd Child—Would He like my old doll with the broken nose?
I could find Him that, and some of her clothes.

Mother *(shaking her head)*—No, children, no, this is not what I planned.
He doesn't want gifts that are secondhand.

(Silence as the children look at each other, puzzled.)

4th Child—Then what does He want? What does He need?

Mother—Ah! That's a very good question, indeed!
He wants daily kindness and daily prayer;
He wants us to work together and share.
He wants us to love our neighbors and friends—
Not just one day, but until the year ends.

1st Child—I understand I'll try harder, you'll see.

2nd Child—I will, too. You can count on me!

Smallest Child *(hugging Mother)*—
I'm only a child, but I'll do my part.
Do you think Jesus would like my heart?

Mother—I know He would! Let's bow our heads and sing a prayer together!
(Group sings "Into My Heart")

Baby Jesus

(Each child carries a card that together spell out "Baby Jesus")

B—Born in a stable, our risen Lord

A—Ascended to heaven above

B—Binding our souls with a golden cord,

Y—Yoking our hearts with His love.

J—Jesus brought love that was undefiled,

E—Every child knows this is true.

S—Songs of the Savior so meek and mild

U—Unveil His love for me and for you;

S—Sweet Jesus, like us, was once a child.

—Gladys M. Seiders

GRADED PROGRAM MATERIAL

Ages 9-11

Star Shine

All the world was still
  On that holy night
When above a hill
  Shone a star's bright light.

Now in winter's snow
  On a Christmas tree
A star's soft glow
  Speaks of Christ to me.

—Gladys M. Seiders

Joy in the Morning

Joy in the morning—everywhere joy!
Shepherds are kneeling to welcome a boy!
Here in a stable on Christmas morn,
At last, the Prince of Peace is born!
Mary, His mother, sings Him to sleep
Amid gentle cattle and white, wooly sheep.
See how He lies in His manger bed
With softest hay to cradle His head!
Come, worship the King. Draw near where He lies
While angel voices resound through the skies!
The world is waiting, and hushed, and stilled,
For the biblical prophecy is fulfilled!

—Jean Soule and Mildred Johnson

A Family Recitation

FATHER—

No room for Jesus in my work—
  Too rough the life for Christian man.
The stories told, expressions used
  Would not fit in the Savior's plan.
    No room for Jesus there!

SON—

No room for Jesus in my play;
  It's worldly pleasure that we seek.
We haven't time for serious things
  Or for a life that's humble, meek.
    No room for Jesus there!

DAUGHTER—

No room for Jesus in the school;
  Too busy there to let Him in.
And we would have to honest be,
  And wouldn't dare to think of sin—
    We don't want Jesus there!

MOTHER *(sadly)*—

No room for Jesus! Oh, how sad!
  He has declared eternally:
"I have no room for those in heaven
  Who have no room on earth for me!"
    No room for Jesus here on earth—
    No room for sinners, there!

—E. L. Russell

The Story of Christmas

By Alma C. Peacock

(Opens with manger scene: Mary, Joseph, and Baby)

There is a town called Bethlehem,
  And there's a story true
About a Babe named Jesus
  Who was sent for me and you.

Mary was His mother's name—
  He was God's only Son.
God sent Him down from heaven above
  To save us, every one.

(Person holding star enters from rear. Insert flashlight for effect.)

Now there were wise men from the east
  Who saw a shining star;
They knew at once it was a sign
  Sent to them from afar.

(Wise men come from rear; walk slowly toward Nativity scene)

They knew the star so bright and clear
  Out in the eastern sky
Would lead them to the Savior-King—
  They'd find Him by and by.

(Star-holder stops over manger—Group sings "Away in a Manger")

The star went on before them
  Until it came to rest
Over the place where Jesus lay
  So quiet and so blest!

(Wise men stop at manager and look down)

There in a lowly manger
  Lay the Savior of all men.
The precious Son of God came down
  To save us from our sin.
And they went in to worship Him.
  They gave Him gifts so rare!
Then they went back to their own home
  The wondrous news to share.

(Group sings a witness chorus.)

The Journey

By Jean Soule and Mildred Johnson

Characters—

FOUR CHILDREN *to make the journey (pretending to walk)*
THE INNKEEPER, MARY, JOSEPH, *and the* BABY (for tableau)

UNISON—Let us go to Bethlehem,
To Bethlehem afar.
Let's be like the shepherds
Who followed one bright star!

1ST CHILD—But how shall we get to Bethlehem?
And what is there to see?

2ND CHILD—I've heard the news—a Babe is born!
Born to make us free!

3RD CHILD—Then let us go to worship Him,
Before that Star grows dim!

4TH CHILD—Don't walk so fast! I'm small, you know.
These rocks are sharp! I stubbed my toe!

1ST CHILD—All is well. I see an inn!
This is the place where the shepherds have been.

2ND CHILD—Yes, this is the place. I see a great light—*(points)*
There in the east—a wond'rous sight!

(Children stop at inn and knock on imaginary door. Innkeeper grumbles crossly)

INNKEEPER—What do you want? There's no room today.
Be off! I haven't a place you can stay.

2ND CHILD—We have heard great news. A child has been born
Here at your place on Christmas morn!

INNKEEPER *(puzzled)*—Not here! Not here! Run along with you;
I'm a busy man. I have things to do! *(Shuts door.)*

3RD CHILD—Hush! Did you hear a baby cry?

4TH CHILD—It came from the stable—there on high.

1ST CHILD—There is the star right over that place!

2ND CHILD—Let us hurry to see the Christ child's face!

(Scene shifts to stable, tableau of Mary, Joseph, and baby in a manger. Children enter and walk slowly and silently to the manger.)

3RD CHILD *(whispering)*—Here's the One we seek, in a manger bed!
Here's the straw where He lays His head!

4TH CHILD—Hush! He is sleeping. Don't make a sound!

1ST CHILD—At last—the Holy Jesus is found!

SONG *(by group or audience)*—"Away in a Manger"

The Christmas Tree

(Seven children, placing ornaments on a tree.)

1ST CHILD—Tonight we'll celebrate the birth
Of Jesus our Savior, come to earth;
Now join us, as our tree we trim!
We do all this to remember Him!

2ND CHILD—Upon the top we'll place a big star,
And think of the wise men who came from afar.

3RD CHILD—And now, as this bright gold ball I lift,
We'll think of the gold they brought as a gift.

4TH CHILD—This candy cane, shaped like a shepherd's crook,
Reminds us of those who were privileged to look
On the Baby's face, that wonderful night—
The Lord of all love, the Lord of all light.

5TH CHILD—This angel will help us remember the one
Who announced to those shepherds the birth of God's Son.

6TH CHILD—And this dove of peace, a gentle bird,
Will help us remember the heavenly choir's word:
"Peace, peace on the earth, good will unto men;
For the Savior is born in Bethlehem!"

7TH CHILD—This lovely bell stands for music and joy,
And all for the birth of a dear baby Boy!

—*Anna Marie Dahlquist*

The Road to Bethlehem

A Pantomime in Two Scenes

by Katherine Paxon

Characters—

NARRATOR

ISAAC—an old man dressed in long robe, turban and sandals

REBECCA—a woman dressed in flowing robe with scarf over head and shoulders, sandals

ESTHER—a woman, dressed similarly to Rebecca

JOSEPH—a carpenter, dressed in long robe, sandals

MARY—a young woman dressed in long, flowing robe, preferably blue or white and scarf of lightweight material draping her head and shoulders

EZRA—a burdened traveler, dressed in rough material long robe with sleveless tunic over it—sack, staff, sandals

INNKEEPER—dressed in short robe, belted tunic, sandals

THREE SHEPHERDS—dressed in robes similar to Ezra

THREE WISE MEN—dressed in brightly colored robes, crowns

THREE WISE ONES—in modern dress

SINGERS—off platform

Any number of children dressed as men and women, boys and girls of biblical times can be participants to create the feeling of crowds along the road to Bethlehem. Each character mentioned in the poem has been given a name to aid actors' sense of identification.

Scenery

Scene One takes place along the road from Galilee to Bethlehem. A few well placed rocks, bushes, and small trees can indicate the out-of-doors. The inn doorway stands at right front of platform.

Scene Two takes place in the inn stable. The same wood structure for the inn door can be used for stable door. The manger straw and doll is placed back from the doorway.

Props

Scroll for Narrator
5 Shepherd crooks or staffs
Large rocks
Bushes, small trees
Cardboard donkey

Rope or reins for donkey
Burlap sack for burdened traveler
Inn doorway and stable entrance—wood assembled to represent front of inn and stable.
Manger, with straw
Bright star
Doll, in manger
Stools for Mary and Joseph to sit on
Wise men's gifts—golden box, two odd size jars
Wise ones' gifts—symbolic gifts, chosen during class discussion

Music Needed

O Little Town of Bethlehem—4 stanzas
O Come, All Ye Faithful—3 stanzas

The Pantomime

Scene One opens with the Narrator standing at front left of platform. Isaac, an old man, is leaning heavily on his staff and hobbling along slowly. Rebecca and Esther and other travelers are already along back of platform, gesticulating to each other as if in conversation. Note—All movement on stage takes place from left to right in this scene.

Narrator reads from scroll as Isaac pauses to rest.

The road is rough,
the hillside steep,
and I am tired
as I slowly creep
along the road
to Bethlehem.

As Narrator begins the second stanza, Rebecca, points to Mary, as Joseph leads the donkey very slowly along the road, shakes her head, showing concern. Esther nods in agreement with Rebecca, during third stanza.

Upon an ass
a young girl rides
her body cradling
an unborn Child
along the road
to Bethlehem.

Tall and lean
a strong man strides
beside the girl,
and gently guides
her stumbling beast
to Bethlehem.

Ezra enters, appearing to be muttering angrily to himself. He is carrying a sack over his shoulder and walking with a staff. The Narrator continues.

Caesar Augustus
has proclaimed
a tax, and we must pay
where we were born
or else be shamed;
and so we walk this road
to Bethlehem.

The rich men can ride
as in a dream . . .
while we poor ones
trudge in never ending stream
from Galilee
along this road
to Bethlehem.

Joseph is center stage now, appearing pensive, and still pulling the donkey. Narrator continues reading from scroll.

We hadn't thought
this way to start
a wedded life
of heart to heart
by taking the road
to Bethlehem.

Too much to bear . . .
the Child, the tax,
the trip; yet I must
keep this bumbling beast
straight in his tracks
along the road
to Bethlehem.

The Narrator pauses, to indicate passage of time, and Joseph continues toward the inn door where the Innkeeper is standing. Narrator continues—

"At last! We're here,
Mary, in our town.
Let's rest awhile . . .
Innkeeper! Have you a room?"
The host turned Joseph down
then offered him a stable stall.
He said, "All beds are full tonight
in Bethlehem."

Lights on the stage are turned out while scene is shifted. Singers off stage sing "O Little Town of Bethlehem."

Scene Two opens with Mary and Joseph either side of the manger, front right of platform. A glowing spotlight shines on them. A bright star reflects the light, extreme right of platform. The Narrator reads—

A brilliant star
lights up the sky
above the inn
and from a manger bed
a baby's cry
is heard with joy
in Bethlehem.

As the Narrator continues reading, three shepherds come quickly from back of auditorium, left aisle facing platform, and kneel before the holy family at the manger. On their way, they point to the bright star and seem to converse.

The weary mother,
her face aglow,
and Joseph's awe
begin to show
how glad they reached
a sheltered place
in Bethlehem.

The three wise men have been traveling down the center aisle toward the manger scene, and now kneel and present their gifts. The wise ones have also been approaching the platform from the right aisle facing the platform, arriving on the platform after wise men present their gifts. They kneel and present their gifts for Jesus while the Narrator reads the last stanza.

The ancient seers
foretold this holy night . . .
and wise ones kneel today
as they did long ago,
before Christ's light
when they arrive
in Bethlehem.

After the last stanza is read, the cast and singers join the audience in singing "O Come, All Ye Faithful."

Christmas Eve Around the World

(Exercise for six children dressed in national costumes.)

1ST CHILD *(Narrator—regular clothes)*—

Around the world on Christmas Eve
We Christian children celebrate
The birth of Christ, who came to earth
That He might open heaven's gate.

2ND CHILD *(dressed as Guatemalan or Mexican Indian)*—

In Guatemala, after we
Have said our poems, just like you,
We eat tamales, spicy hot,
Under the skies when church is through.

3RD CHILD *(dressed in pajamas and night cap)*—

In Sweden, we are all in bed,
For we must rise before the dawn
To go to early morning church
And thank the Lord for His dear Son.

4TH CHILD *(holding out pair of shoes)*—

In Brazil, for gifts, we set shoes out—
We don't use stockings, as you do.
And though we sing in Portuguese,
Our carols tell of Christ's birth, too.

5TH CHILD *(dressed as African)*—

No snow in Kenya on this night,
But where flame trees their branches lift
We gather in our village church
To sing of Jesus, God's best gift.

6TH CHILD *(dressed as Russian, radio to ear)*—

In Russia, we are not allowed
To go to church, as you do here;
But on the radio which we hide,
The Christmas message comes in clear.

(All six children put down what they are holding and join hands as they recite:)

Together on this Christmas Eve
We clasp our hands, and say as one,
"God bless us all this holy night
As we remember His dear Son!"

—Anna Marie Dahlquist

The Pine Tree's Prayer

(One child recites while others decorate or add a few decorations to platform tree.)

Dear Lord, these decorations
Have given me a clue,
And now I really understand
The reason why I grew;
To give great joy and happiness
To all who look on me,
Reminding them of Jesus' birth
And His life in Galilee.
The star that tops my highest branch
Is but a tiny spark
Compares to Thy bright countenance
That lights the world so dark;
While the blessed Child of Bethlehem,
Thy Son, the Savior dear,
Gives forth a radiance so divine
It shines both far and near.

—Gladys M. Seiders

GRADED PROGRAM MATERIAL

Junior High

Pooh Bear Learns About Christmas

By Sally Pentecost Boyd

Cast

CHRISTOPHER ROBIN (C. R.)
POOH
NANNY
PIGLET
EEYORE
KANGA
ROO
RABBIT

Optional Pantomime:

MARY
JOSEPH
SHEPHERDS
ANGEL OF THE LORD
ANGELS
WISE MEN

Production Notes:

This play, based on the familiar A. A. Milnes characters, is designed to be flexible for use in large or small groups. The eight Pooh caracters have script to memorize, with Christopher Robin and Pooh having the more lengthy parts. Should the participants be limited in number, the narrative may be accompanied by projected pictures of the familiar Christmas story rather than pantomime. If this option is used, the children may draw the pictures, which in turn can be photographed and processed into 35-mm. slides.

Larger groups may wish to add music to the pantomime scenes. Such numbers as "Angels We Have Heard on High," "Away in a Manger," or "What Did You Say Was the Baby's Name?" might be sung by older children or junior high teens.

This is an ideal presentation for junior highs to produce as a special Christmas gift to the children of the Sunday School and church. Young teens will have great enthusiasm for this special project. Begin planning soon enough in advance that the teens will be able to have input regarding scenery, costumes, and so on.

In an opening announcement to the children in the audience, it may be wise to remind them that while the wonderful characters of Pooh and his friends are imaginary and for fun, the story of Jesus' birth is true, and the characters involved there really lived.

Costuming:

CHRISTOPHER ROBIN—wears short pants, a short-sleeved shirt, white socks, and tennis shoes.

NANNY—long dress with white apron; little frilly maid's hat made of heavy drawing paper and lace.

Animal heads, hands and feet—

Plan 1: Simplicity 9050 as a guide for head, hands, and feet (exclude rest of body in pattern).

Plan 2: Omit hands and feet costuming. Staple appropriate construction paper ears to a paper headband.

POOH—Yellow or gold head, hands, and feet. Ears short and rounded; yellow or gold pajamas or sweat suit with short red vest.

PIGLET—Pink head, hands, and feet; ears—short and pointed; pink pajama bottoms or pants; brightly striped T-shirt; circular chenille wire tail.

RABBIT—White head, hands, and feet; white jeans with white knit top or white sweat suit; pink or white pom-pom tail.

EEYORE—Grey or blue head, hands, and feet; ears, long and dangling; blue pajamas or sweat suit with dangling tail with bushy fringe on end.

KANGA—Brown head, hands, and feet as above; ears: short and pointed; long curving tail, touching floor. Curve tail by sewing cloth into long, thin triangle, turning it, and filling with a bent clothes hanger and polyester stuffing.

ROO—made like Kanga, only smaller.

Note: The A. A. Milne stories, from which these characters were taken, are published by E. P. Dutton & Co., Inc., and copyrighted.

Scene: *A small tree decorated with cranberries and popcorn is at the left of the platform. Christopher Robin and Pooh are adding new popcorn to it.*

POOH—Now why is it we are tying popcorn to this little tree, Christopher Robin?

CHRISTOPHER ROBIN (C. R.)—Because it's Christmas, Pooh!

POOH—Oh. I thought that, Christopher Robin, but, I mean, well, I'm a bear of little brain, and I meant . . .
(Pooh is interrupted by carolers and Christopher Robin's excited response)

C. R.—Listen, Pooh! Carolers!
(Carols sung either by small group or recorded, offstage)

POOH—I wish I could make up hums like those!

C. R.—Thank you, thank you! *(Carolers exit)*

POOH—Is this because of Christmas, too, Christopher Robin?

C. R.—Why, yes, Bear, it is, of course.

POOH—Well, why do people sing at Christmas, Christopher Robin? And why do we tie popcorn on trees?

C. R.—To celebrate, Pooh. To celebrate!

POOH—I see, Christopher Robin, and why is your mother so busy baking so many of those fancy cookies, but you don't eat them?

C. R.—For the people who stop in to see us, Pooh.

POOH—They must be awfully hungry! That's a lot of cookies!

C. R.—Oh, you silly old bear! They're for presents! Little plates of cookies for presents!

POOH—I saw a whole pile of presents with ribbons *(motioning with arms wide)*, Christopher Robin, and I don't know who's having the birthday. It can't be yours, because we had it just a little while ago.

C. R.—Oh, we all get presents at Christmas, Pooh, we all get them. I have to get one for Nanny, too. I haven't figured out what she'd like.

POOH—You mean you give presents, too, Christopher Robin? You get presents and you give them at Christmas? Why?

C. R.—Well, Pooh, it's like this . . .

NANNY *(poking head through doorway)*—Oh, Christopher; Christopher Robin!

C. R.—Right here trimming a tree for the birds, Nanny.

NANNY—Come, Christopher, it's off to the post office to mail all these cards. Oh! I've finally finished! I'm glad Christmas comes only once a year. Hurry! We have to get ready to go to the party, too. I have to hem your pantlegs.

C. R.—Well, I guess I have to go, Pooh. Enjoy our tree with the birds! *(C. R. and Nanny exit.)*

POOH—Pretty little tree. *(walking about tree, admiring it)* Kind of lonely without Christopher Robin . . . So busy now that it's Christmas. I wonder what ever started Christmas? . . . hasn't had time to tell me! Carolers, song about a baby, hay, Jesus, heaven, love—How I wish I knew! *(Goes stumping out door a few moments, comes back in, talking excitedly to Piglet, waving arms and moving head to emphasize words)* . . . and then a bunch of kids came and they were singing about Jesus. And Christopher Robin's mailing a bunch of cards with Nanny, and he's going to have a party. And he doesn't know what to give Nanny—and there are bunches of presents, and . . .

PIGLET—Pooh! Pooh, look! Look at this new kind of tree! It grows red things *(tastes one)*—yuk! They don't taste like haycorns and . . . and . . . popcorn?

POOH—That's what I mean, Piglet! It's another crazy thing Christopher Robin says is because it's Christmas. He puts popcorn on trees!

PIGLET—Wow! Whatever it is, Christmas really is mysterious! We usually pick things off trees, not put them on.

POOH—So you don't know what it is, either?

PIGLET—No, I sure don't. Not even my grandfather, Trespassers W., ever told us anything like this, Pooh!
(Enter Eeyore, noisily, gloomily.)

PIGLET *(frightened)*—Hey, what's that, Pooh?

Eeyore—It's not a *what's*, it's a *who's*?

Pooh and Piglet—What? *(jumping a little)*

Eeyore—Who!

Pooh—Oh, Eeyore, it's you!

Eeyore—Yes, Pooh, Piglet—It's me, Eeyore. And a *me* is a *who*, not a *what*.

Pooh *(while Piglet stands openmouthed, calming down)*—What is a who—I mean a me is a who or a . . . Oh, I get it. Yes, Eeyore, you're a who, I see. Hello!

Eeyore—Hello, Pooh. Hello, Piglet. Yes, even though it seldom crosses anyone's mind, I am a who. A who rarely thought of.

Pooh—Oh, we think of you, Eeyore, we do! We were just wanting to ask you, weren't we, Piglet, if you can tell us what Christmas is.

Piglet—Yes, yes. Pooh and I were. Eeyore, tell us, what is Christmas? Do you know?

Eeyore—Christmas? Well, it doesn't belong to the thistle family, or I'd have heard of it for sure.

Pooh—Oh, no, Eeyore, no! It's to celebrate! It's sort of like birthdays. They give presents, have parties, send cards, sing . .

Eeyore—Well, why ask me? No one remembers a donkey for parties and such. *(Kanga and Roo enter from right, Roo hopping quickly ahead.)*

Kanga—Roo, dear; no, Roo! Oh, sometimes I wonder what ever forces me to force strengthening medicine down you! Roo!

Roo *(reaching Pooh and friends)*—Hi, Pooh! Hi, Piglet! Hi! Mother, I've found Pooh and Piglet!

Eeyore—*And* Eeyore. No one ever cares that they've found Eeyore!

Others in chorus—Oh yes, we do! Eeyore, we do!

Kanga—My, my, such a lovely sight! Whatever is this? *(Roo runs clapping, dancing, and pointing at the tree)*

Pooh/Piglet—Oh, Kanga, it's a Christmas tree, and we hope you know. What is Christmas, Kanga?

Kanga—It must be a kind of pine, I guess. I've never seen one before.

Pooh—No, no, Kanga! Christopher Robin got it by the six pine trees. It's a regular tree. He did it! *(He looks at Piglet, who nods in agreement.)* Christmas is to celebrate. And they sing. It's about a baby Jesus. Have you heard about Him?

Kanga—No, not even in hopping school. No, I haven't.

Piglet—Oh, who will ever tell us? Christopher Robin is so busy with it, he'll never have time.

POOH *(scratching head)*—I know. Let's ask Rabbit! He has real brain!

(They all move toward right side of stage, Piglet scurrying ahead)

PIGLET *(knocking on door)*—Rabbit; oh, Rabbit! Come quick! Tell us what Christmas is!

(Rabbit comes out. As he talks, the group walks back toward the tree.)

RABBIT—Christmas is, uh, let's see. I think I remember some of my friends and relatives mentioning it. Seems they sing—and they have parties.

(Every time he says something, the others say, "Yes, yes," "Go on," or "We know that!")

RABBIT—And let's see. They fix these fancy trees. *(looks up)* Why, I'll be! Yes, sir! Just like that right there.

ALL—We know, Rabbit, we know! But what else is Christmas?

RABBIT—I don't know. No, I don't rightly know.

EVERYONE—Oh. *(Quietly, as in deep disappointment; just then Christopher Robin swings in the door merrily, waving)*

C. R.—Hey, I'm back, Pooh! *(Looks about)* Hi everyone! What don't you know, Rabbit?

POOH, PIGLET, and ROO—He doesn't know more about Christmas than we know.

POOH—And all we know is people sing and give cards, go to parties and fix up trees, and get presents—and the songs are about a baby Jesus.

C. R.—Oh, Bear! I need to tell you, don't I? And you, Piglet and Roo.

EEYORE *(firmly)*—And Eeyore! Donkeys like to know, too!

C. R.—Oh, yes; yes, of course, Eeyore, you need to know. And Kanga and Rabbit! Come sit down. *(Motions)* It's a long story. *(They all sit by the tree, stage right.)* It all started long ago.

POOH—Before you were born, Christopher Robin?

C. R.—Oh, yes, Pooh! Long, long ago when there were no electric lights and no TVs or airplanes. Long, long ago before there were cars!

EVERYONE—Wow!

PIGLET—You mean before dinosaurs, Christopher Robin?

C. R.—Well, no, Piglet, but not too long after Abraham and those guys lived in tents.

EVERYONE—Oh! *(awestruck.)*

(This part may be taped ahead by Christopher Robin or he may read it. The Christmas pageant may either be pantomimed or projected on a screen stage left. Lights down on Pooh characters at this time, and up on Christmas scenes.)

C. R.—God had promised He would send His Son, a Savior, so His chosen people, the nation of Israel, were waiting and waiting for Him to be born. Their country was ruled by Rome, and they had to pay lots of taxes to

Caesar, who was a harsh ruler. *(Pantomime or project picture of Bethlehem, with Mary and Joseph walking.)*

God had told a young girl before she was married she was going to have a baby who would be the Son of God. She and Joseph, her husband, had to go to Bethlehem to pay their taxes just when God's Son was ready to be born. They were poor, so Joseph and Mary had to walk and ride a donkey. *(Eeyore perks up, motions to the others to notice.)* It was a long way. When they finally got there, it was late at night. They were so tired! But they had no place to stay. An innkeeper—that's like a motel keeper—let them stay out where the animals slept—sort of like in the garage, except the animals were kept there. In a barn. *(Pantomime or project picture of Mary, Joseph, and the manger.)*

And while they were there, God's Son was born! They named Him Jesus. The stable was not like a hospital at all. It was cold and dirty . . . Not at all the kind of place you would expect God to have His Son born. *(Pantomime or project picture of shepherds in their fields by the fire.)*

And God chose unusual people to tell about His Son. He didn't tell the king, like our president, or even the city council. He told shepherds. While they were watching their sheep, the angel of the Lord came. *(Project angel and have someone speak words, or if pantomiming, have the angel come out and speak.)*

ANGEL—Fear not! For behold I bring you glad news of great joy for everybody! For to you is born today in the City of David a Savior, which is Christ the Lord.

(Optional—angel choir may sing at this time)

C. R.—*(Project or pantomime manger scene with shepherds.)* So the shepherds ran to Bethlehem and found Mary, Joseph, and the Baby.

People far away who knew God's children for many years, had also known that they were expecting a Savior. *(Project or pantomime wise men)* Wise men saw a bright star God sent to celebrate His birth. *(Wise men look at the star and discuss it together.)* The star must have been very special, to get so much attention! It was very unusual! They decided to go see God's Son. We don't know how many wise men came. Probably several. They brought three gifts to Jesus: gold, frankincense, and myrrh—gifts given to kings in those days. They worshipped Him and returned home.

(Lights up on Pooh characters.)

EVERYONE—What a beautiful story!

EEYORE—And they even used a donkey to carry the mother of God's Son!

C. R.—Yes, they did, Eeyore!

POOH—I've thought up a hum! Oh, help me sing it, Piglet and Roo!

(They hold hands to sing a Christmas song.)

NANNY *(coming in)*—Oh, Christopher Robin, you know the story so well!

KANGA—Let's really celebrate!

EVERYONE—Yes, let's sing! *(All cast sings "Joy to the World.")*

POOH *(Turning to audience)*—Please join with us!

The Baby in a Manger

by E. L. Russell

Cast

Five junior highers posing as adults; one young boy. Barefoot, robes.

Men wear turbans; women wear headscarves. Abijah, the child, is hump-backed.

A voice from offstage will be needed at the end of the play.

Setting—

All three acts take place in the family living room, low couches or mats on the floor, Middle Eastern style. It is census time in Bethlehem and all the city is filling up.

Act One

FATHER—The inn is filling rapidly, and in an hour there won't be any rooms left at all. People are arriving early to find a place to stay.

ABIJAH—Couldn't we let some guests have my room? I'd gladly sleep in the stable if we could show hospitality to some weary traveler.

MOTHER *(patting him on the shoulder)*—You forget one thing. Uncle Zebedee will be coming in and he will have to share your room. He will be very tired after his long trip.

ABIJAH *(excited)*—Of course! How could I forget? *(Looking at his mother quickly)* Uncle Zebedee can have my bed!

FATHER—This taxation is such a burden for those who have moved a long distance from where they were born. Rome has no mercy, and Cyrenius, governor of Syria, is pleased the way people are responding.

ABIJAH—I met a family from Capernaum today. I'm glad we never moved from the place our forefathers lived.

FATHER—Yes, we are fortunate. But the travel does offer opportunities for new experiences and new friends.

ABIJAH—I didn't need to travel to find new friends.

FATHER—Our neighbors have already taken guests in. I wonder what latecomers will do.

MOTHER—They should have come earlier if they wanted to get rooms.

FATHER—True. But some must travel farther and besides, some, with little children or old people in their party, must move more slowly.

Neighbor *(appears at open door)*—Hail, friends! May I come in?

Father—Peace be with you, Levi! Enter in love! *(He comes in.)*

Neighbor—Do you have any room to spare?

Father—No. My brother Zebedee will arrive any minute. We promised him a place during the census.

Mother—Is there someone seeking a place?

Neighbor *(nodding his head)*—Yes, and they need a room right away. The woman is about to have a baby. Their journey had to be slow and painful from Nazareth.

Abijah *(as his parents shake their heads)*—Couldn't they use the stable?

Mother—I wish we could do something.

Abijah—The stable wouldn't really be bad.

Mother—You don't suppose they would . . .?

Neighbor—They seem very simple folks, humble and God-fearing. I think they would appreciate it.

Father—So be it, Levi. Abijah has slept there often.

Mother—Maybe I can be of help when the time comes.

Father—I'll go and extend the invitation. *(He leaves with Levi.)*

Abijah—May I go, too, Father?

Father *(from offstage)*—Yes, Son, it was your idea. Mother, could we share our evening meal?

Mother—Of course. I'm not very hungry anyway.

Abijah *(as he is leaving)*—Abraham entertained angels centuries ago. I wonder if we're going to entertain angels?

Act Two

(The setting is the same. Uncle Zebedee has joined them.)

Mother—They seemed so appreciative of our hospitality.

Father—It was better than nothing. I just wish we had been better prepared for them.

Uncle—You might have waited until some higher class travelers came along. I don't think this couple can reward you very well.

Father—Now, Zebedee, you know us better than that. I'm simply loaning to the Lord, and He will repay.

Mother—Mary was so happy to find a place to rest. The journey was a real hardship for her.

Abijah—I hope she bears a son!

MOTHER—All children are a heritage of the Lord, but a son would be nice. Levi said she told him it would be a son.

ABIJAH—God told her?

FATHER—She is either a prophetess or a dreaming mother.

UNCLE—Or a witch or a demon.

MOTHER—You wouldn't say that if you had talked with her. I'd better go and be there in case she needs me.

ABIJAH—Let me go, because I should feed the animals and carry straw anyway.

UNCLE—You won't get any thanks for all this. Wait and see.

MOTHER—I have all the thanks I need—a good husband and a son that is precious to my heart. If they can have a child who is as obedient as Abijah has been, they will be greatly blessed.

NEIGHBOR WOMAN *(rushing into the room)*—It's a boy!

MOTHER *(standing up, shocked)*—So soon?

NEIGHBOR—Yes, so soon! She's wrapping him now in swaddling clothes!

MOTHER—I must go see if I can do anything for her! *(Women leave together.)*

FATHER—Too bad they couldn't get in at the inn, but at least they are protected from the weather. They are sheltered and comfortable.

ABIJAH—God gave her the boy she wanted.

ZEBEDEE—A lot of mothers want sons and don't get them. How do you account for that?

ABIJAH—Mary is special. I know it.

FATHER—God gave your mother the son she wanted, too.

ABIJAH—My mother is special, too.

ZEBEDEE—Such talk is sickening. I'm going for a walk. *(He leaves.)*

ABIJAH—I'm glad I wasn't born to Zebedee.

FATHER—Be careful, Son. We ought not to judge like that. Maybe a son like you would have helped him to believe. We must pray that he will have more faith.

ABIJAH—I do. I pray for Uncle Zebedee every night.

FATHER—Then we must believe God will lead him into faith again.

Act Three

(Same setting. Abijah is standing near the door. Father and Mother are seated.)

FATHER—What did you say happened?

ABIJAH—Shepherds came to the stable and knelt down before the Baby. As they were leaving they told that angels had appeared to them.

FATHER—You talked with the shepherds?

ABIJAH—They talked with me. They said the Baby was the long-awaited Messiah!

MOTHER—Can this be true?

FATHER—You mean they said this Baby is the Messiah?

ABIJAH *(nodding)*—Yes. They said the angels told them they would find the Baby in the manger, and that He was the Messiah!

FATHER—And did you go see for yourself?

ABIJAH—I want to go see the Baby, but I wanted to ask you first. May I go?

FATHER—Yes, Son. But remember there are false teachers and there will be false messiahs as there have been in the past.

MOTHER—But the right One will come, and this could be the One.

ABIJAH—It is the One! *(He hurries away.)*

FATHER—I hope our son isn't being deceived. It seems too much to ask to think the story is true.

MOTHER—Aren't you going to find out for yourself?

FATHER—Of course. But Abijah has such faith. I thought we should see what he learns. If he is disappointed, we should be here to comfort him. *(Abijah rushes in. His hump is gone.)*

ABIJAH—Mother! Father! Look! My hump . . . my hump is gone! *(They jump up and examine him.)*

MOTHER—Son! What happened?

FATHER—It's gone! Your hump is gone!

ABIJAH—When I went in and bowed down to worship the Baby, as the others there were doing, my body became straight! *(Turns around as they continue to examine him, showing emotion.)* I felt strength in my body I have never felt before. Oh, Mother! This is the Messiah! It was His way of thanking us for the stable!

MOTHER—Surely this must be the Messiah!

FATHER—Let us thank the Lord for what He has done for our boy before we go, too, to worship the Messiah. *(They freeze in prayer posture.)*

READER OFFSTAGE—"For unto you is born this day in the city of David a Saviour, which is Christ the Lord. And this shall be a sign unto you: Ye shall find the babe wrapped in swaddling clothes, lying in a manger" (Luke 2:11-12).

Make Room for Jesus

A Christmas Reading with Pantomime

By J. C. Leatherman

Cast:

NARRATOR	SHEPHERDS
MARY	WISE MEN
JOSEPH	HEROD
CAESAR	SIMEON
INNKEEPER	ANNA

Pantomime:

As the reader comes to each biographical sketch, the character(s) described enter(s) side door and moves to center stage, where he (they) stand(s) momentarily, either profile or full-faced to the congregation. Spend enough time on costuming to make the character convincing. When the sketch is finished, the character(s) exits through the opposite door. At the proper time, all characters in cast file back across the platform in procession, reentering the original door.

The Reading

One very fascinating thing about the birth of Christ was the number and diversity of people whose lives were touched. They were drawn as though by a magnet into the drama that became the dividing point of history. Each played his part; some willingly and knowingly, others reluctantly or ignorantly. Those who had a part in this historical pageant were lifted out of obscurity, forever immortalized in the pages of sacred and/or secular history. The course of their lives was altered. No one, having been in contact with the Christ child, remained the same.

Each had his moment, and his part to play. For that moment he occupied the center of the stage; then moved aside to make room for another. Finally, all disappeared from the scene and left only the Son of God, to occupy the spotlight alone. The others were but a supporting cast. The real Star appeared and will forever remain the chief attraction.

Let us open the pages of sacred writ and note briefly some of the supporting actors.

ENTER MARY. First, there was Mary, a young woman possibly in her teens. She was of humble, but noble, lineage. Her devotion to God and her obedience to His will were unquestionable. She was discreet and chaste in her conduct and became a willing partner with God in bringing His Son into the world. She made occasional appearances on stage during the life and ministry of Jesus and for a time thereafter. *EXIT MARY.*

ENTER JOSEPH. Then there was Joseph, a just and devout man. He, too, was of royal descent, although he worked at a humble but honorable vocation. He was a carpenter. Joseph was a patient man, close enough to God to hear Him speak—and having heard from God, was quick to obey. Joseph was a good man who had an important part in the Nativity and early life of Jesus. Then his name fades from the record, to be seen no more. *EXIT JOSEPH.*

ENTER CAESAR. Caesar Augustus—though he didn't know it—played a small but important part in the plot. He was emperor of Rome, and Rome controlled the Mediterranean world. Caesar decreed that all should be taxed, which meant that everyone had to be enrolled. Without Caesar's decree, Jesus would have been born in Nazareth, but the census brought Joseph and Mary from Nazareth in Galilee to Bethlehem in Judea. Caesar's part was perfectly timed, so the Child was born in Bethlehem as the Scriptures had foretold. *EXIT CAESAR.*

ENTER INNKEEPER. The innkeeper has played a part in Christmas tradition simply because every inn must have an attendant. He is not mentioned in scripture, and perhaps some of the criticism laid on him because he didn't provide a room in which Mary could have her baby may be unjust, too, for we are not told that. Actually, he was just an ordinary businessman or employee doing his job. Even today it would be considered proper business ethics to take your customers impartially as they came, unless, of course they had a reservation. He could not very well turn out a guest who was already occupying a room. The inn was full. Giving the use of the stables was, in reality, an act of kindness for which he shall be remembered. *EXIT INNKEEPER.*

ENTER SHEPHERDS. As with the innkeeper, no names are given to the shepherds who came. Just shepherds. Ordinary, nameless, working men. Undoubtedly they were devout men who cherished the hope of a coming Messiah. To them was given the privilege of first hearing the good news of great joy and of being the first witnesses of Christ. Theirs was a very dramatic part, but one that was very fleeting. *EXIT SHEPHERDS.*

ENTER WISE MEN. Other nameless participants who played a significant role were the wise men from the East. These were not the ordinary working men of the Orient. They were called Magi. Some have suggested they were kings, but more likely they were astronomers or priests. They were deeply religious men who knew Jewish prophecies pertaining to the coming Messiah. The time they had determined; they were only waiting for the sign. Their travel involved preparation and risk, expense and endurance—and yet they came. Isaiah had prophesied, "and the Gentiles shall come to thy light and kings to the brightness of thy rising." Having paid their homage, they faded into oblivion as mysteriously as they had appeared. *EXIT WISE MEN.*

ENTER HEROD. Every play has a villain, and so it was on this occasion. Herod, the Idumean, was a puppet king over the Jews, who derived his authority from Caesar. He was mean and treacherous and would not hesitate to slay his own mother or sons when he supposed them to be plotting for his throne. A man of his perfidious nature could not tolerate another in his kingdom who was called

"King of the Jews." His order to execute Bethlehem's infants was in keeping with his character. *EXIT HEROD.*

ENTER SIMEON. There was an elderly man named Simeon in Jerusalem. He was a godly man who had the Holy Ghost and who waited for the consolation of Israel. The Holy Spirit had revealed to him that he would not die until he had seen the Lord's Christ. Joseph and Mary took Jesus to the Temple on His eighth day, as was the custom, for circumcision and dedication. Simeon was led of the Spirit to come to the Temple at the very time Jesus was brought in. Upon seeing Jesus, he knew immediately that God had fulfilled His promise. Simeon took the Infant into his arms and praised God. He uttered prophetic words concerning Jesus and Mary which she never forgot. Simeon was now ready to depart this life in peace. *EXIT SIMEON.*

ENTER ANNA. And then there was Anna, a prophetess who practically lived at the Temple. She served God night and day with fasting and prayer in spite of the fact that she was 84 years old. The widow came into the Temple when Jesus was being presented unto the Lord. She also gave thanks and spoke of Him to all who looked for redemption in Jerusalem. *EXIT ANNA.*

PROCESSION OF CHARACTERS ACROSS STAGE. All these and many more played a role in the pageantry surrounding the birth of Jesus. They are but typical of multitudes who came in contact with the Lord during His life, His ministry, and His death. They represent all walks of life, all cultures, all levels of society. These were men and women, Jews and Gentiles, noblemen and peasants, rich and poor, learned and unlearned, old and young, housewives, politicians, scholars, laborers, businessmen and professionals, conquerors and conquered religious and irreligious, devout and profane. One thing they all had in common—at some time in their lives they came in touch with Jesus.

This is a continuing experience, for He is that true Light that lights every person who comes into the world. In His ministry He stated that if He were lifted up He would draw all men unto Him. He came to call all men and women everywhere to repentance.

Sooner or later, every individual must reckon with Him. In the ranks of His followers are to be found laborers and managers, students and professors, laymen and ministers, soldiers and generals, citizens and public officials, infants and senior citizens, illiterates and Ph.D.s, paupers and philanthropists, New Guinea bushmen and English royalty. All have come to Jesus and have found the encounter the most important event of their lives. They were born, they lived, worked, studied, laughed, loved, built homes, enjoyed friendships, had family ties, and ultimately will die—but the one event that stands out above all others is their encounter with Jesus. He is their hope, their joy, their reason for living.

The student is challenged to devote his mental acumen to His service. The toiler works with purpose, doing even menial tasks for His glory. The housewife sings for joy, for she serves not only her family, but her Lord. He challenges the youth, sustains the adult, and comforts the aging.

Jesus is the Star arising out of Jacob, the Lily of the darkest valley, the Rock of all ages, the Sun of righteousness arising with healing in His wings. He is the Wonderful, the Counselor, the Mighty God, the Everlasting Father, the Prince of Peace. Truly of His government there is no end. He is altogether lovely, He is the Good Shepherd, the Bread of Life, the Light of the World, the Friend of sinners—the Lamb of God and the Coming King. He is indeed the Christ, the Son of the living God!

Contact with Jesus is electrifying, but in itself is not sufficient. We must *receive* and *accept* Him. The shepherds came and departed glorifying and praising God, but the rich young ruler came, and went away sorrowful. The wise men followed the star with exceeding great joy, while Herod grew more hateful and violent. Simeon prayed, "Now let thy servant depart in peace, for mine eyes have seen thy salvation," but the chief priest and elders cried, "Away with Him—let Him be crucified!"

Pilate asked a question that is still pertinent: "What shall I do then with Jesus which is called Christ?" As he was confronted with this decision, so also are we. What will our answer be? The proper course may be found in John 1:10-13 (NIV). *(Read this portion.)*

Before the season passes, lay hold upon His promise. Like Thomas, give up your doubting and claim Him as your Lord and your God; like Zacchaeus, come down out of your tree of self-effort and let Christ come into your heart and home; like the woman at Sychar's well, ask for the water of life so you shall never thirst again. Like Peter, leave all and follow Jesus. Like the man who found the treasure in a field, sell all you have with joy, and buy that field. Like Bartimaeus, call upon the Lord until your eyesight is restored. Like the thief on the cross, confess your sins and plead for mercy.

As we celebrate once more the wondrous event of Jesus' birth, make room in your heart for Him. Do it now, will you?

SPECIAL NUMBER: "Have You Any Room for Jesus?"

Across the Road

A Christmas Skit

By Carol Costa

Cast

NARRATOR
PETER, JANE, and MARTHA *(rich children)*
BILLY and JENNY *(poor children)*
DAD and MOM *(poor)*
TRAVELER and TRAVELER'S WIFE *(Middle Eastern costumes)*
TOWNSPEOPLE *(rich and poor people)*

Costumes—
Poor people and travelers wear tattered clothing. Rich people dress up with jewelry, etc.

Props—

Shawl

Blanket with holes

Crust of bread

Basket with food

Doll, to represent the Baby King

Setting—

Divide any stage in half. If spotlight is available, lights up on the side of the street where the action is.

At rise—

Billy and Jenny are on the poor side; Peter, Jane, Martha, and extras are on rich side of town. The narrator is standing in the middle.

NARRATOR—Once upon a time, in a faraway land, there was a tiny village. A winding road, which ran right through the middle of it, divided the town in half. On one side of the road the houses were large and very elegant, while on the other side, they were small and not so nice.

It is a cold winter night and in a large house, the people are preparing for a party. They have heard that a king is coming to their town tonight.

PETER—How do you like my new clothes? I got them just for the party tonight. I wanted to look nice for the king.

JANE—I think mine are much nicer, especially this lovely new shawl I'm wearing. It was very expensive.

PETER—Well, it's okay I guess, if you like that color.

MARTHA—Stop arguing and come and help me with the food. Besides you both know that my clothes are the most beautiful. Fit for a king, if you know what I mean.

JANE—What kind of food are we having tonight?

MARTHA—Turkey, roast beef, potatoes, salads—I've had the servants preparing for days. Nothing but the best.

PETER—Why do you need help? Where are your servants?

MARTHA—They begged me for the night off to be with their families. Don't worry, they'll be back extra early to clean up in the morning.

(Scene switches to poor side of town)

BILLY—It's awfully cold in here. Should I put another log on the fire?

JENNY—Dad said to wait until Mom gets home. That's all the wood we have. Come over here and I'll share my blanket with you.

BILLY—Well, okay. *(He moves towards her.)* But I don't see what good it will do. Your blanket is full of holes.

JENNY—I hope Mom was able to get some food from her boss. They always have lots of extra, especially when they're having a party.

BILLY—That reminds me. Besides being cold, I'm hungry too.

JENNY—I saved a crust of bread from this morning. You can have it. *(She reaches into her pocket and hands it to him.)* Look out the window at that beautiful star.

BILLY—Is that the star that means that the king is coming?

JENNY—I don't know, but just looking at it makes me feel warmer.

BILLY—Well, if a king does come to this town, one thing is for sure.

JENNY—What's that?

BILLY—He won't stop here unless he wants to freeze to death. *(There is a knock on their door.)*

JENNY *(calling out)*—Dad, there's someone at the door. *(Dad enters and goes to door, he finds a man and woman standing there.)*

DAD—Yes, can I help you?

TRAVELER—My wife and I have been traveling many hours and are very cold and tired. Could we please come in and warm ourselves by your fire?

DAD—Please come in. Your wife looks very pale, is she sick?

TRAVELER—No, not exactly. She just needs some rest.

DAD—While we're waiting for my wife to come home, the children and I will go out and try to gather more wood for the fire. Please make yourselves at home.

JENNY—You can use my blanket. *(She holds it out and TRAVELER'S WIFE takes it.)*

TRAVELER'S WIFE—Thank you. It's a lovely blanket.

(Scene switches to rich side.)

PETER—I thought I heard someone at the door. Who was it?

MARTHA—Just a couple of travelers asking for shelter. I sent them away.

JANE—It's a good thing you did. If the king came in and saw those two ragamuffins, I'd be embarrassed to death.

PETER—Yes, and you wouldn't want to be caught dead in that dress you're wearing. *(Everyone begins fighting and yelling.)*

(Scene switches to poor side. Mom enters carrying a basket of food on her arm.)

MOM—Children, I'm home. *(Seeing travelers)* Oh, Who are you? Where is my family?

TRAVELER—They went out to gather more wood. My wife isn't feeling well and they were kind enough to let us in to rest. I hope it's all right.

MOM—Of course it is. We don't have much to offer, but perhaps I could make her some tea.

TRAVELER'S WIFE—You're very kind. If I could just lie down for a while.

MOM—My boss gave me some extra food tonight, and we will gladly share it with you. Please be our guests for supper. *(Scene switches back to rich side.)*

MARTHA—Now that everyone has stuffed themselves with food, I hope you'll be in better moods. What will the king think if he finds us all fighting?

JANE—If he were coming, he should have been here by now. It's way past dark.

PETER—He probably heard that you were here, and decided not to come.

JANE—How dare you!

MARTHA—Stop fighting! *(Soft music begins playing.)*

PETER—Do you hear that music?

MARTHA—Look out the window. There's a beautiful star shining over the house across the road. It looks like all the poor people are gathering there. *(Extras for poor side of town begin entering and gather around the Traveler and the Traveler's Wife.)*

JANE—You don't suppose that the king got lost and went to that side of town by mistake?

PETER—I don't know but I'm going over there and find out.

MARTHA—Wait for me. *(All rich people go across to other side.)*

MARTHA—What's going on here?

BILLY—A baby boy has been born to the travelers, right here in our house.

JENNY—It was wonderful. As soon as the baby was born the house was lit up with warmth and light, and this beautiful music started. Everyone is saying a King is born.

MARTHA—May we see Him?

DAD—Of course, everyone is welcome. *(The poor people move aside to show the Traveler and the Traveler's Wife. She is cradling a baby in her arms.)*

PETER—He is beautiful. Thank you for letting us see Him.

JANE—Yes, and I wouldn't want Him to ever feel cold. Here, please take my shawl to wrap Him in. *(She removes her shawl and gives it to the Traveler.)*

MARTHA—Let's go back and get all that food, that's left over, to share with these people. From now on we will share all that we have.

JANE—We'll be so busy sharing and helping each other that we won't have time to fight and be unhappy.

NARRATOR—And so our story ends. This season, may the joy of our newborn King bring all people together. The warmth and light of love are there for all of us, sometimes, just across the road.

We Have Seen the Baby

S. T. Steve Tippett

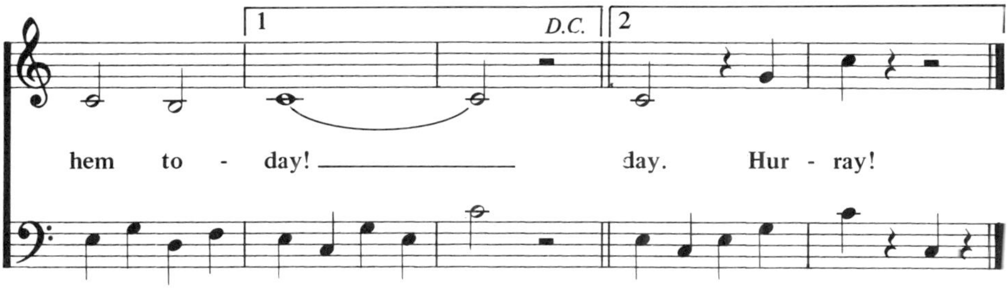

What Is That Strange Sound I Hear?

E. K. E. | Ernest K. Emurian

Gloria Deo

Anon., alt. by L. L.

Lyndell Leatherman

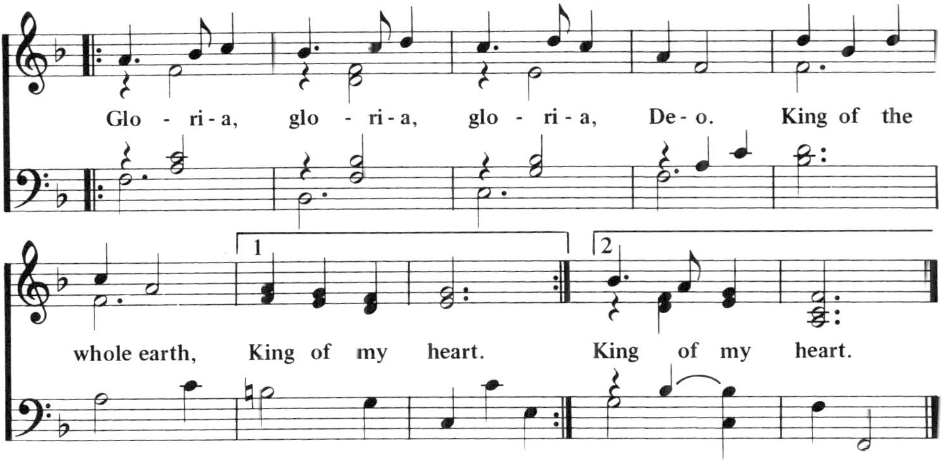

Little Baby Jesus

P. J. A.

Patricia Jean Alderson

A Seasonal Wish

R. M. | Robert Miller